# Priorities

## Mastering Time Management

# Resources for Changing Lives

A Ministry of
THE CHRISTIAN COUNSELING AND
EDUCATIONAL FOUNDATION
Glenside, Pennsylvania

RCL Ministry Booklets
Susan Lutz, Series Editor

# Priorities

## Mastering Time Management

James C. Petty

**P&R**
PUBLISHING
P.O. BOX 817 • PHILLIPSBURG • NEW JERSEY 08865-0817

© 2001 by James C. Petty

Printed in the United States of America

ISBN 10: 0-87552-685-3
ISBN 13: 978-0-87552-685-0

It was 7:45 on a Saturday morning. Bill lay there, paralyzed. Who was he going to displease today? His wife? His boss? The deacons at church? His kids? His own conscience?

Bill had no easy answers. As a Christian, he knew that he could not just "cop out" on the callings God had given him as worker, husband, father, church member, adult son, and Christian. He really did want to walk worthy of his calling and please his Savior.

So he steeled his mind against the images of the beautiful, trout-filled reservoir where he had fished every afternoon prior to his marriage six years ago. Bill was alarmed at the amount of jealousy he was feeling towards his unconverted fishing buddies. They were probably there now . . .

That feeling scared him enough to make him roll quickly out of bed, get dressed and prepare to spend another day hopelessly doing the impossible. He would try to live up to the commitments he thought were part of his Christian life.

I have met many people like Bill, and they need help. I know, because at times I have been Bill myself. This booklet tackles the issues of priorities and time management using the Assessing My Priorities (AMP) Worksheet, a tool designed to help Christians do two things. First, it will help you to identify clearly and specifically the "oughts" in your life—the things you assign yourself as priorities. Second, it will help you to compare the time needed for those priorities with the time that God has actually given you—and to consider any adjustments you may need to make.

## Living Under Priorities, Not Pressure

The AMP Worksheet was developed to help Christians apply Paul's teaching in Ephesians 5:15–6:18. Paul is speaking to the issue of godly priorities and time use when he says,

> Be very careful, then, how you live—not as unwise but as wise, making the most of every opportunity, because the days are evil. Therefore do not be foolish, but understand what the Lord's will is.

While it may seem that this passage just adds to the sense of commitment overload, it actually affords a very freeing way to deal with the time pressure-cooker. In this passage:

1. Paul teaches that the development and exercise of thoughtful discernment ("Be very careful, then, how you live") is the key to enabling Christians to deal with time-use decisions.
2. The challenge is for Christians to "redeem" (KJV), buy up, or use the opportunities God has given them before his return.
3. This is especially important since the days are evil. We live in the period of history where the final battle with evil is underway.
4. Wisdom helps us to understand God's will by connecting the management of our time and opportunities with what is important in light of eternity and Christ's kingdom.
5. Paul pleads for believers to bring time use, along with every other aspect of life, under the control of the Spirit. Otherwise we will be controlled (filled) by alcohol or some other life-controlling force.

## Applying the Principles

In Ephesians 5:18–6:18, Paul applies his teaching by identifying the core priorities in each major area of life. These core priorities are framed as positive commands, which are applications of the great command to love God and love one another as he has loved us. Since they are mostly positive commands, we need wisdom to connect them to the circumstances and people in our lives. They are commands that cannot be reduced to a list of prohibited actions or even a universal "to do" list.

The areas Paul identifies are as follows:

- *Worship and fellowship (Eph. 5:19–20).* "Speak to one another with psalms, hymns and spiritual songs. Sing and make music in your heart to the Lord, always giving thanks to God the Father for everything, in the name of our Lord Jesus Christ."
- *Church functioning (v.21).* "Submit to one another out of reverence for Christ."
- *Marriage (vv.22–33).* "Each one of you also must love his wife as he loves himself, and the wife must respect her husband."
- *Duties of children (Eph. 6:1–3).* "Children obey your parents. . . ."

- *Parenting (v.4).* "Fathers . . . bring up [your children] in the training and instruction of the Lord."
- *Employees (vv.5–8).* "Slaves, obey your earthly masters. . . . serve wholeheartedly, as if you were serving the Lord. . . ."
- *Bosses (v.9).* "Masters, treat your slaves in the same way. . . ."
- *Personal spiritual priorities (vv.10–18).* "Finally, be strong in the Lord and in his mighty power. Put on the full armor of God. . . ."

Although Paul does not cover every area of life (political responsibility, Sabbath rest, etc.) he does identify the core values in these major areas.

Through Paul, the Holy Spirit reminds us that the Christian life is a life of multiple priorities. Notice that Paul does not allow us to decide which of these areas of life should take priority over any other area. He does not say, for instance, that your marriage comes before work, or that worship comes before marriage, or that personal spiritual growth comes before child rearing. He does not see these core values as a list of responsibilities arranged in either descending or ascending order.

Biblically, we are not permitted to decide to which areas of life we will apply the commands of God. They must apply to *every* area. Nor may we prioritize *between* the commandments of God. In every area of life and service, we must avoid prohibited thoughts, motives, and actions, and positively pursue the things God calls us to do. In other words, Paul wants us to fulfill our first priorities in *every* area of life before we fulfill lesser priorities in any area. A first priority in any area would take precedence over a second or third priority in any area.

Looked at from the perspective of time management, this means that we should make sure we have completed all our first priority activities in every area of our calling *before* we begin scheduling second priority activities. In the same way, second priorities should be fulfilled before we move on to third priorities. For example, a priority of family does not mean that a father can leave his job early whenever his son has an after-school basketball game. To do so would be to give one area of life priority over another, and to give a lesser activity priority over a first level activity. Let's illustrate how this way of thinking could help Bill.

# Wisdom for Bill

Here are some steps that Bill could take, using the AMP Worksheet, to assess his feelings of overcommitment and see if they reflect reality. If he finds that he is overcommitted, he can then look for ways to bring his life into conformity with God's priorities and will.

STEP 1. First, using a blank AMP Worksheet and a pencil with a good eraser, Bill lists every activity he believes he ought to be doing to please the Lord in every area of his life. Some people may be organized enough to keep a log of activities and times for a few days to help them be realistic. Below are the kinds of activities Bill thought about and listed. He used three major headings: (1) God, (2) God's people, and (3) God's work in the world. Other ways of organizing the list can also be used; this particular list is only a suggestion.

## Focus on God

- Preparation for public worship
- Personal Bible study and meditation
- Personal prayer and worship
- Christian books, tapes, and TV programs
- Spiritual retreats and conferences

- Public worship (including transportation time)
- Family worship
- Worship and prayer with spouse
- Small group worship & fellowship (including transportation time)
- Sunday school class
- Other

# Focus on the People of God

## Stewardship of self
- Sleep—minimum and optimum amount
- Eating, meal preparation, and clean-up
- Personal hygiene, dressing
- Exercise
- Relaxation, entertainment, TV, video, movies, Internet
- Reading paper, magazines, mail, catalogs
- Sports, hobbies

## Family Relationships
- Spouse—minimum and optimum amount, talking, "going out," fun, helping
- Children—reading, playing, talking, teaching, and discipline
- Family activities—playing, talking, fun
- Parents—mine

- Parents—spouse's
- Other relatives
- Transporting family
- Children's activities

## Household work and service
- Chores, housecleaning, cooking, laundry
- Errands, banking, gas, auto care
- Bill paying, taxes
- Repairs and renovations

## Friendships
- Discipling friendships (include phone time)
- Other Christian friendships (include phone time)
- Dating (if not married; include phone time)

## Ministry
- Ministry responsibility in church, include prep time
- Other Christian organizations, schools, missions
- Personal ministries—not organized

# Focus on God's Work in the World

## Job
- Time required for basic job, lunch and transportation

- Job responsibilities or overtime beyond that

**Non-Christian friends—list names**

**Community and political service**
- Political party
- Service clubs
- Diaconal help to those outside the church
- Volunteer jobs
- Social clubs

**Evangelistic ministries and missions to non-Christians**
- Within the church or denomination (evangelistic meetings, other outreach programs)
- Parachurch ministries (evangelistic Bible studies, rescue missions)
- Personal ministries (friendship evangelism, deeds of mercy to neighbors)
- Miscellaneous—categories that do not fit above.

STEP 2. Beside each activity, Bill indicated the relative priority of that activity. He chose from four possible priorities: (1) An absolute, non-negotiable priority; (2) An important priority; (3) A priority that is good when possible; (4) An activity that is clearly optional.

STEP 3. Beside every activity, he wrote on the worksheet how much time he should devote to that activity in a four-week period (28 days). The AMP requires Bill to add in 35 hours (5%) next to miscellaneous to allow for the general mess and inefficiency of life, opportunities God brings along that cannot be scheduled, and the need for some margins in any life.

STEP 4. Bill added up the total hours required in a four-week period to fulfill all these activities. He then determined how much difference there is between his expectations and the 672 hours available in four weeks. (This exercise also could be done just for work hours by reducing the time to work hours alone, and listing work activities only.)

STEP 5. Bill's total was over 672 hours, so he went back through his list to cut out activities that are "clearly optional." His total still exceeded 672 hours, so he cut out activities that were "good when possible." He was still over 672, so he started cutting out important activities, trying to harmonize with the 672 hours available.

STEP 6. The column on the right of the worksheet leaves room for notes regarding each activity and what action is needed to get information, talk to specific people, or make changes in your schedule. If Bill, for instance, finds it difficult to decide what to cut, he can go back though Paul's teaching in Ephesians 5:18–6:18 and meditate on the core priorities taught there. He could also enlist the help of his spouse, pastor, or friends. Very often these folks have unique and helpful perspectives on what is really important and what only appears to be. Sometimes we need help in letting go of less important activities. Often we are getting something unhealthy out of the activity and need help breaking the hold of some idols of our heart. These can involve the fear of man, the need for success, recognition, safety, control, money, attention, affirmation, winning, confidence in one's own righteousness, and many other desires that can gain control of our hearts and displace God.

This exercise can help followers of Christ grow in discernment as they explore which activities are most important in each of their relationships. For example, many wives would rank the priorities in God's command, "Husbands, love your wives," very differently than their husbands would. The same is true of God's word to wives, "The wife must respect her husband." Bosses sometimes have a different view of the proper priorities of an employee's work. The same can be true of parents to adult children, pastors to church members, and even friend to friend.

Underneath the drive to bring Bill's self-expectations ("oughts") into line with the time God has allowed was the bedrock belief that God never gives us more than he expects us to do in the time allowed. That must empower our faith as we seek to discern the non-negotiable from the important, the good, and the optional. Paul prays for the Philippians that their "love may abound more and more in knowledge and depth of insight, so that you may be able to discern what is best" (Phil. 1:9-10).

This discernment can be sought and developed so that we can accurately assess God's will in our priorities and schedules. It enables us to live in his will with greater integrity. It brings with it the fruit of greater peace (about not doing everything), greater confidence about what we choose to do, and a renewed motivation and joy to realize that with the Spirit's discernment, the Christian life is possible to live from a time use perspective. To be sure, God asks us to do things in our schedules that are impossible ("Love your enemies"), but he sovereignly and graciously provides all the time we need to fulfill his will.

## Priorities for Bill

When Bill first filled out his AMP Worksheet, he found that he had 875 hours of expectations for himself against 672 actual hours available in the month. He was shocked that his expectations and God's expectations were 200 hours a month out of sync. He was 200 hours out of the will of God!

Bill ended up going to his wife and pastor and asking for help. They came back with suggestions for cuts and exchanges in the "Important" category. They recommended that Bill resign from two ministries in the church (Sunday school teaching and budget committee) and to concentrate instead on his role as a deacon, with a particular focus on leading the financial counseling ministry within the church. The pastor even helped Bill make some phone calls to cancel commitments that he had unwisely made.

The three of them honed Bill's priorities and hours until he had time to be home or with the family four nights a week. His wife had found herself increasingly exhausted from her part-time job when she also had to manage the home by herself in the evenings. They all agreed that Bill should have at least one of those nights to focus on in-depth communication and prayer with his wife. They added one night a month for friendship with non-Christian friends and neighbors, and they also decided that half-day fishing trips are important for Bill every month or so. Another addition was a fun night out every month for Bill and his wife as a couple—with dates set in advance to keep them from being crowded out by other commitments.

Bill's revised AMP (shown on pp. 18–21) still reflected some twenty hours of illegitimate "oughts"—because he either had too many activities or too much time given to some of them. But at least now he was reasonably close to the 672-hour goal. He could now continue to refine his commitments to move toward 672 hours.

At first Bill was a little depressed about canceling some commitments to concentrate on others. He felt like some kind of traitor—

particularly to the ministries he was quitting. But slowly he entered into his new priorities with much more motivation and creativity. He found his heart more engaged with these activities because he knew they were possible to do well and because he knew he was much closer to doing the will of God.

## Other Applications

Perhaps Bill's problem is not your problem at all. Perhaps you are on the other end of the spectrum, where you feel underchallenged and unproductive, and you are concerned that you are wasting too much of your life. The AMP Worksheet can also be helpful for you. It can lead to a fruitful consideration of the rich Scriptural teaching on the need to be stewards of our time. It can help you as a believer to avoid idleness or to drift into priorities that focus on leisure, self-indulgence, riches, personal isolation, escape and a host of other pitfalls. Whatever its use, I hope that it will be a practical help to Christians learning to obediently live by priorities, and not pressure or self-oriented pleasure.

Paul the Apostle prayed that God would fill the Colossian believers with "the knowledge of his will through all spiritual wisdom and understanding" (Col. 1:9). Paul prayed this prayer so that these believers may "live a life worthy of the Lord," please him in every way, and bear fruit in every good work (Col. 1:10). Whatever your present situation, may this prayer also be fulfilled in you.

*This booklet is adapted from the Appendix to my book,* Step by Step: Divine Guidance for Ordinary Christians *(Phillipsburg, N. J.: P & R Publishing, 1999). For an exposition of the principles underlying biblical guidance, including time use, please refer to this book.*

**James C. Petty** *is a counselor and the director of the Children's Jubilee Fund in Philadelphia.*

Bill's Assessing My Priorities Worksheet

| Activities | Relative Priority | | | | Time | Changes Needed |
|---|---|---|---|---|---|---|
| List All Your Activities | Non-negotiable | Important | Good when possible | Clearly optional | Hours required in 28 days | How to make needed changes |
| Personal worship, devotions | x | | | | 4 | |
| Family worship | x | | | | 4 | |
| Small group fellowship | x | | | | 6 | |
| Prayer with spouse | x | | | | 4 | |
| Church and Sunday school class | x | | | | 12 | |
| Sunday reading | | x | | | 4 | |
| | | | | | | |
| Sleep—minimum | x | | | | 196 | |
| Sleep—additional | | | x | | 14 | |
| Dress, wash, clothes | x | | | | 7 | |
| Exercise | | x | | | 6 | |
| Eating—breakfast, dinner | x | | | | 28 | |
| Relax—TV, "A" | | x | | | 12 | |
| Relax—TV, "B" | | | x | | 12 | |
| Reading, paper | | x | | | 12 | |
| Sports league | | x | | | 4 | |
| House repair | | x | | | 4 | |
| Bills, taxes, bank | x | | | | 4 | |
| | | | | | | |

| Activity | | | | Value |
|---|---|---|---|---|
| Weekly conference with spouse | x | | | 8 |
| Communication with spouse (daily) | x | | | 14 |
| Going "out" | x | | | 3 |
| Relaxing with spouse | x | | | 14 |
| Help with chores, shopping | | x | | 14 |
| Children—talking, reading | x | | | 14 |
| Kids sports | | x | | 4 |
| Family activities | | x | | 12 |
| Parents | x | | | 8 |
| Friends | | x | | 4 |
| Primary ministries | x | | | 20 |
| Secondary ministries | | x | | 5 |
| Rotary club | | x | | 4 |
| Job—basic | x | | | 180 |
| Job—extra time | | | x | 20 |
| | | | | |
| | | | | |
| | | | | |
| | | | | |
| | | | | |
| Miscellaneous | | | | 35 |
| Total Time Required | | | | 692 |
| Time Provided | | | | 672 |
| Difference | | | | 20 |

# Assessing My Priorities Worksheet

| Activities | Relative Priority | | | | Time | Changes Needed |
|---|---|---|---|---|---|---|
| List All Your Activities | Non-negotiable | Important | Good when possible | Clearly optional | Hours required in 28 days | How to make needed changes |
| | | | | | | |
| | | | | | | |
| | | | | | | |
| | | | | | | |
| | | | | | | |
| | | | | | | |
| | | | | | | |
| | | | | | | |
| | | | | | | |
| | | | | | | |

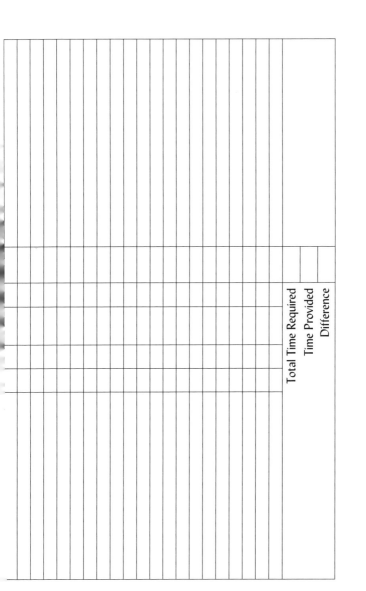

| | | | | | | | | | | | | | | | | | | | | | | | |
|---|---|---|---|---|---|---|---|---|---|---|---|---|---|---|---|---|---|---|---|---|---|---|---|
| | | | | | | | | | | | | | | | | | | | | | | Total Time Required | |
| | | | | | | | | | | | | | | | | | | | | | | Time Provided | |
| | | | | | | | | | | | | | | | | | | | | | | Difference | |

# RCL Ministry Booklets

Booklets by Jeffrey S. Black, Michael R. Emlet, Walter Henegar, Robert D. Jones, Susan Lutz, James C. Petty, David Powlison, Paul David Tripp, Edward T. Welch, and John Yenchko.

| | |
|---|---|
| *ADD* | *Pre-Engagement* |
| *Anger* | *Priorities* |
| *Angry at God?* | *Procrastination* |
| *Bad Memories* | *Prodigal Children* |
| *Depression* | *Self-Injury* |
| *Forgiveness* | *Sexual Sin* |
| *God's Love* | *Stress* |
| *Guidance* | *Suffering* |
| *Homosexuality* | *Suicide* |
| *"Just One More"* | *Teens and Sex* |
| *Marriage* | *Thankfulness* |
| *Motives* | *Why Me?* |
| *OCD* | *Why Worry?* |
| *Pornography* | *Worry* |

See all the books and booklets in the Resources for Changing Lives series at www.prpbooks.com